INTRODUCTION

THE BOOK THAT ISN'T A BOOK

THE SECRET HISTORY *of the* ZOHAR

The Kabbalah Centre
155 E. 48th St., New York, NY 10017
1062 S. Robertson Blvd., Los Angeles, CA 90035

First Edition
October 2008
Printed in USA
ISBN10: 1-57189-611-2
ISBN13: 978-1-57189-611-7

Design: HL Design (Hyun Min Lee) www.hldesignco.com

www.kabbalah.com™

THE

SECRET
HISTORY
of the
ZOHAR

MICHAEL BERG

TABLE OF CONTENTS

To all outward appearances, it fulfills the requirements of a book. It sits serenely on the shelf, paper neatly bound and sewn, with print and leather, but the *Zohar* is not really a book. According to the kabbalists, this is the energy and Light of the Creator—condensed, packaged, and made available to every human on Earth. And while it could be said to have been "written," actually that would be less than accurate, since the *Zohar* was *revealed*.

The revelation of the *Zohar* ("splendor" in Hebrew) occurred in a cave in Judea some two thousand years ago. The man who received this revelation was Rabbi Shimon bar Yochai, a luminary in the lineage of Kabbalah. So what is this book that is not a book, which was revealed rather than written, and which offers its power to us so many years later through the letters of an obscure, ancient language? It is an encyclopedia of secrets, a compendium of virtually all our knowledge of the Universe. It is an explanation of the spiritual architecture of reality: codes and metaphors through which we understand the purpose of life and learn to transcend the limitations of this physical world.

The *Zohar* takes the form of commentary on the Bible, through conversations among spiritual masters. These masters are often portrayed as being on a journey, sharing speculations about passages from the Bible, with their discussions culminating in sudden flashes of insight or revelation; thus each character in the *Zohar*, along with their purposes and destinations, is charged with meaning. All the journeys, of course, are really one journey—the same one we are making in the course of our lives—and all depict characteristics of various aspects of ourselves. In this sense, and also as a literary work, the *Zohar* is fascinating and rewarding. But as vast and valuable as that is, the *Zohar* is inherently far more precious because, most significant of all, the *Zohar* is constructed of Light; its history is a chronicle of the revelation of the Light of the Creator in this physical world.

This may sound like hocus-pocus. And it would be if the *Zohar* were simply a book. But this is the book that isn't a book—it is a user's guide to life. And I am blessed with the opportunity, now, to share with you the unique, secret history of the *Zohar* and its effects on humanity as we know it.

A trinity of texts

At the heart of Kabbalah lies a great trinity of texts. The first of the trinity, *Sefer Yetzirah* (*Book of Formation*) or *Book of Abraham*, was revealed four thousand years ago to no less an author than Abraham, the Biblical Patriarch. In its few scant pages, incomprehensible to most people, the *Book of Formation* describes the physical and metaphysical nature of the Universe and the formulas of Creation—formulas rendered not in numbers but in Hebrew letters. According to the *Book of Abraham*, the twenty two letters of the Hebrew alphabet are actually twenty two distinct energies, each with its own numerological significance and domain of Creation. These are described by kabbalists as the very engines of Creation, the DNA of the Universe.

The second text in the trinity appears four centuries later: the Bible, revealed to Moses after the exodus from Egypt. Kabbalists view the Bible as a manifestation of the Creator's Light, but like the *Book of Formation*, so compressed as to render it all but incomprehensible (if taken at face value), to the untrained reader.

More than a thousand years would elapse before the revelation of the third in this trinity of texts, the key that would unlock the previous two: the *Zohar*. The *Zohar* is the soul of the Bible, and they are as inseparable as our own souls are from the bodies that house them.

Aramaic

The *Zohar* is written in the ancient language of Aramaic. Largely forgotten, Aramaic, a sister language to Hebrew, employs Hebrew letters. It was spoken two millennia ago in the land that is now Israel, and several books of the Old Testament were written in Aramaic. But whereas Hebrew was the language of the upper class, Aramaic was the language of the common people. Why, then, was the *Zohar* revealed in this, the common tongue, rather than in Hebrew?

The kabbalists teach that Light reveals itself in a manner that may appear counter-intuitive. For Light to be revealed there must be a Vessel to receive it. Desire is a Vessel; so the greater the desire for the Light, the larger the Vessel and the more Light will be revealed. The only thing that limits revelation of Light is a lack of desire on the part of the receiver. Thus we arrive at a basic, although seemingly illogical, kabbalistic concept: The lower the Vessel, the greater the Light it can reveal. Because a lower Vessel is further from the Light, it has a greater desire for the Light. Thus Aramaic was the chosen language of revelation for the Light of the *Zohar*; because it is the lower language, with the spiritual ability to reveal the extraordinary Light.

And then the *Zohar* speaks of a second reason for Aramaic.

> *Aramaic is above any invisible negative influences and this language provides a direct connection to the Creator. Accordingly, when the Creator reveals important wisdom that requires protection from potentially harmful angelic forces, the wisdom is expressed in Aramaic.*
> —*The Zohar, Lech Lecha 27:287*

Kabbalah explains that angels are forces of energy, both positive and negative, that exert powerful influences over our lives. The Aramaic language is a protected habitat from the angels, because the angels do not "recognize" it. Indeed when the Creator wanted to speak to Abraham and ensure that no angels awakened judgment on him, the Creator chose to speak in Aramaic.

Since the time of Creation, Aramaic has been a language that can both reveal great Light and provide protection. The *Zohar* was revealed in the language of Aramaic, the language of the common man rather than of the more refined Hebrew, and so this is a message to us that this tool of Light can and should be used by all people, regardless of their spiritual level. The more disadvantaged a person is spiritually, the more important it is for this individual to use the *Zohar*, for the *Zohar* is the one spiritual tool that can reach anybody, anywhere.

There is a final significance to the Aramaic language. Aramaic employs Hebrew letters, so the Light of the *Zohar* glows with the very letters Abraham depicted as the energies of Creation, the forces that built the Universe. Thus, the words of the *Zohar* are not merely words; they are the actual mechanism by which we connect to the Light of the Creator. Without the Aramaic text, the *Zohar* would simply be a book of wisdom, an instruction manual for a telephone without the telephone itself.

The invisible history

Before the Creation, before there was a physical world, before there were dimensions, before time and space, the Light of the Creator spread always and everywhere. Thus begins the kabbalistic history of the Universe written by the great twentieth century kabbalist Rav Ashlag. In *Talmud Eser Sefirot* (*Ten Luminous Emanations*), Rav Ashlag's commentary on the writings of Rabbi Isaac Luria, the Light was everywhere and the essence of this Light was to give, to share. But in order for this sharing to take place, something had to exist that could receive the Light. A receiving entity, which kabbalists call the Vessel, was thus created.

At one point in the primordial environment the Light withdrew to create the space for the receiving Vessel to come into being, and then the Light flooded back into the Vessel. But when it did, the Vessel shattered under the impact, and that shattering created what is now the physical world. (Modern science calls this moment of Creation the Big Bang.) The Vessel shattered into countless fragments, sparks of the Creator's Light that are concealed within all material reality, waiting to be revealed by our actions and our consciousness.

Plants form the base of the food chain—there would be no animal life without plants—and the food they create is synthesized by the action of the sun; therefore, when we eat we are unlocking the sunlight concealed within the food molecules. In much the same way, the Creator's Light has been hidden inside every aspect of reality; and it is up to us to unlock the Light.

"Let there be Light."

According to the *Zohar*, the "Light" referred to is not physical light. It is the source of all the joy and fulfillment that will ever be achieved by humanity, the Light of the Creator. Kabbalah offers humanity a fundamental truth: connection to the Light brings us happiness and total fulfillment; disconnection from the Light brings pain and suffering. This fundamental insight is both simple and profound, but its implications are clear. Our life can have only one goal: ceaseless striving to achieve continuous connection with the Light of the Creator. This connection is the job of the *Zohar*.

Initially, the Creator revealed the Light, but then concealed it in order to give humans a chance to earn that Light through our actions. Where is the Hidden Light (referred to as *Or HaGanuz*) concealed? About this, Kabbalah is also quite clear. The Creator placed it in the *Zohar*.

Since the beginning of time, many tools have been made available to mankind. But only two have existed since *before* the beginning of time: the *Zohar* and the Bible. They exist in a realm outside of time and space, so in a sense they have no origin.

THE
SECRET HISTORY
OF THE ZOHAR

The history of the *Zohar* is everything you would expect of a mystical text—an account filled with intrigue, danger, numerous turns, riddles, and mysteries. It begins two thousand years ago, just after the destruction of the Second Temple of Jerusalem.

THE KABBALIST
SHIMON BAR YOCHAI
(RASHBI 100-160 CE)

Rabbi Shimon bar Yochai, the author of the *Zohar*, was one of the great Talmudic and Torah scholars of the second century. In fact, he was the student and disciple of Rabbi Akiva ben Joseph (50–135 CE), who is considered to be one of the greatest souls to ever appear in physical reality.

Rabbi Akiva was known for seeing only the good in everything. Once, while traveling, Rabbi Akiva could not find overnight lodging in a particular city. He happily spent the night outside the city walls, without complaint. When a lion killed his donkey, a cat ate the rooster that was supposed to wake him at sunrise, and a cold wind extinguished the flame of his only candle, he said: "This too is for a good purpose." In the morning, Rabbi Akiva discovered the truth of his own words. During the night the city had been overrun by an enemy army, which captured all of the citizens and sold them off into slavery. Rabbi Akiva escaped because his sleeping quarters remained hidden by a cover of darkness, and no beast or bird had accidentally betrayed his whereabouts.

Rabbi Akiva was a master scholar of the Bible, including the mystical teachings known as Kabbalah, but it was his student, Rabbi Shimon bar Yochai, who was given the task of revealing the inner secrets of the Bible. When Rabbi Shimon became concerned over his own potential, his master responded that both he and the Creator knew Rabbi Shimon's greatness and that their trust in him should suffice to reassure him.

Still, the question inevitably arises: if Rabbi Akiva was considered the greatest soul to walk this Earth, why was Rabbi Shimon chosen to be the one who would reveal the *Zohar*? The great Rabbi Isaac Luria (the Ari) put it this way:

> *"The sanction to write this book of wisdom was not given to the sages who preceded Rabbi Shimon because, even though they were highly knowledgeable in this wisdom, even to the extent of exceeding Rabbi Shimon, they lacked his ability to encompass and to protect the esoteric lore."*
> —*Writings of the Ari (Kitvei Ari), Vol. 6 p. 91, Gate of the Parables of Rashbi.*

The Slaughter and the Martyr

Unimaginable destruction took place in the second century. It was during this time that the Roman Empire outlawed any form of kabbalistic teachings and Bible study. The great Rabbi Akiva disregarded the prohibition. As a result he was arrested, imprisoned, and eventually skinned alive, the flesh stripped from his bones by the Romans for his continued attempts to ensure that all the people would come to know the ultimate truth of the Bible—*Love Your Neighbor as Yourself.*

The Second Temple in Jerusalem was destroyed in 70 CE and twenty four thousand students of Rabbi Akiva died during this time, wiped out by a plague. According to both Talmudic and Kabbalistic sources, Rabbi Akiva's students died and the Temple was destroyed for only one reason—a lack of tolerance between the students and unwarranted hatred among the Israelite nation. From these tragic events, the kabbalists understood that wisdom was not enough to achieve world peace. Instead, tipping the scales on the side of kindness, selflessness, and mutual respect would determine whether there would be peace or pain in the world.

One of Kabbalah's most important teachings is that, to be successful, any endeavor must have unity among all those involved. Certainly this was true for the revelation of the *Zohar*, which itself describes the unique reality that enabled its great revelation in the time of Rabbi Shimon bar Yochai. Surprisingly, the essence of that reality was not great learning or righteousness but the unconditional, endless love that was present among the friends, as the students of Rabbi Shimon were called.

> *"All the friends during the days of Rabbi Shimon loved each other, soul and spirit. Therefore, in the generation of Rabbi Shimon the secrets of the Torah were unveiled. For Rabbi Shimon used to say: "All the friends that do not love each other cause themselves to deviate from*

the straight path. Also, they blemish the
spiritual wisdom, because the wisdom
has in it love, friendship and truth.
Abraham loved Isaac and Isaac loved
Abraham, so they embraced each other.
Both were attached to Jacob with love
and friendship, and gave their spirit to
each other. The friends must be like
them, and not cause a blemish in them."
—*The Zohar, Ki Tisa 54*

And Then There Were Five

After twenty four thousand of Rabbi Akiva's
students died, only five remained; and among
them, his disciple, Rabbi Shimon. By this time
the Romans had not only outlawed, on penalty of
death, the practice of rabbinical ordination, but
they had decreed the total destruction of any city
where ordination took place. To avoid this
massive destruction of innocent life, the second
century sage Rabbi Yehuda ben Baba shrewdly
took Rabbi Akiva's five students into the hills and
ordained them between two cities, Shefaram and
Usha. Then, as the Roman soldiers were hunting
them down, Rabbi Yehuda told his disciples to
flee.

"What will become of you?" they cried out. He
answered: "I shall place myself before them as an

immovable rock." Rabbi Yehuda ben Baba was struck down by 300 arrows and lances launched by the Roman soldiers. The great sage willingly gave his own life so that Rabbi Shimon and his four colleagues could live.

The Inner Wisdom

Eventually, the Roman Emperor had placed a sentence of death upon Rabbi Shimon, fearing his great power and influence. To escape the Roman soldiers, the great Kabbalist and his son, Rabbi Elazar, took refuge in a cave in Pequi'in. There, for thirteen years, father and son buried themselves in the ground up to their necks in an effort to subjugate the distractions of the body. It was during this time that they received instruction in the deepest mysteries of the Torah from Elijah the Prophet. These teachings would become the foundation of the *Zohar*.

The *Zohar* tells us that although battered and decomposed, Rabbi Shimon was joyful and fulfilled when he emerged from the cave. The difficulty he endured brought great Light to him and to the world.

> *When Rabbi Pinchas went to meet Rabbi Shimon, he saw that Rabbi Shimon had completely changed. His body was*

*full of scars and sores from having stayed
so long in the cave. Rabbi Pinchas wept
with Rabbi Shimon and said, "Woe that
I have seen you so." Rabbi Shimon
replied, "How happy is my lot that you
have seen me so. Because had you not
seen me so scarred, I would not be what
I am."*
—*Zohar Prologue 185*

The cave dwelling and thirteen years both have
mystical significance since thirteen is the
numerical value of the Hebrew word *echad*,
which means one. This alludes to the fact that
during this period Rabbi Shimon achieved
devekut (cleaving or oneness) with the Creator.
The "cave" signifies the inner aspect of the Torah,
and is a common symbol for mystics who enter
into the hidden mysteries of wisdom.

The Revelation of the *Zohar*

Thereafter, Rabbi Shimon gathered his closest
colleagues, known as the *chevarim*—the
brotherhood or the friends—in another cave
located in the Galilee known as the *Idra Rabba*—
the Great Assembly. Here the ten sages gathered
to explore and reveal the teachings given to Rabbi
Shimon during his thirteen-year seclusion in
Pequi'in.

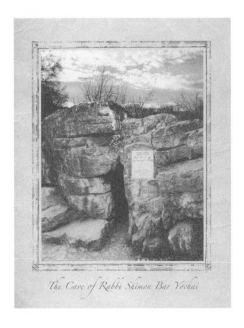

The Cave of Rabbi Shimon Bar Yochai

Rabbi Shimon was clearly torn about whether or not to reveal the *Zoharic* mysteries, for there was a cosmic need to reveal this mystical Light associated with the teachings, but also an equal need to ensure its secrecy. After swearing his initiates to an oath of secrecy, Rabbi Shimon began the revelation. Remarkably, the entire teachings of the *Zohar* were revealed in a single day, even though it had taken thirteen years for Rabbi Shimon to amass this wisdom. Employing the language of metaphor, Rabbi Shimon's discourse explored the hidden inner structure of the Universe and the Secret of God.

Concealing the *Zohar*

One of Rabbi Shimon's disciples, the Kabbalist Rabbi Abba, was a gifted writer with the ability to conceal the innermost secrets of the *Zohar* through allegory and metaphor. Thus the task of committing the *Zohar*'s oral teachings to written word was handed over to him.

Rabbi Yitzchak of Komarno, who described the sequence of the writing of the *Zohar*, wrote in his work, *Netiv Mitzvotecha*, p. 136:

> *"Know, my brother, that the Zohar was written by Rabbi Shimon bar Yochai, and Rabbi Abba his disciple wrote down whatever he had heard, both from him and from the colleagues. Rabbi Abba is the one known (in the Talmud) as Rav."*

Over the next few hundred years, the *seed* that was planted in the *Idra Rabba* was nurtured as the wisdom of Rabbi Shimon's original discourse evolved and developed into the form of a finished set of manuscripts known as the *Zohar*; the Book of Splendor was deliberately hidden for many centuries. According to the teachings of the early eighteenth century Kabbalist, Moshe Chaim Luzzatto (the Ramchal 1707-1746), the original revelation of the *Zohar*, in the *Idra Rabba*, was equivalent to a single drop of Light, providing just enough spiritual Light to sustain the world until such time in the future when the complete revelation of the *Zohar* would bring about the Final Redemption.

As to this long period of concealment, kabbalists refer to the *Zohar's* comments in the section of *Shemot* (Exodus).

> *"The Zohar's teachings were to remain hidden until 1200 years after the destruction of the Second Temple—one hundred years for each of the 12 Tribes of Israel. During this time, in each new generation the wisdom of Rabbi Shimon was passed orally from teacher to disciple. The place the Zohar would reappear was Spain."*

REDEMPTION FEVER

Just prior to the appearance of the *Zohar* in Spain, apocalyptic and messianic predictions were rampant. Pope Innocent III (1161-1216) expected the Second Coming to take place in 1284. Spanish Kabbalist Rabbi Abraham Abulafia (1240-1291) predicted the Redemption of mankind in the year 1290. Rabbi Abraham ben David of Posquieres (the Rabad 1125-1198) forecast the Final Redemption as coming sometime around the year 1216, based on the visitations of Elijah the Prophet. Abraham ben Hiyya (1070-1136), the great astronomer and mathematician, calculated the appearance of the Messianic age in the year 1230. Joachim of Fiore (1135-1202), considered the most important apocalyptic thinker of the whole medieval period, had a series of visions that established 1290 as the "opening of what is sealed and the uncovering of what is hidden." Kabbalist Moses ben Nachman, Maimonides (1194-1270), predicted that the return of prophecy, which would usher in the Age of the Messiah, would take place in 1216.

Such was the climate prior to the revelation of the *Zohar* in Spain.

THE 13TH CENTURY:
THE *ZOHAR* APPEARS

The renowned 19th century scholar Israel Zinberg, considered the foremost historian of Jewish literature, describes the emergence of the *Zohar* in Spain this way:

> *"At just that time an event occurred which is of the greatest consequence not only for Jewish mysticism, but for the further development of all Judaic culture. A great work, a treasury of the*

25

whole Jewish mystical world of ideas, the greatest and most brilliant memorial of the Kabbalah and mystical creativity produced in many generations, suddenly appeared. This monumental work made its appearance wrapped in mystery and wreathed in legends of miracles. It was not a book, but a revelation. And it was revealed not to a common mortal but to the godly Tanna Rabbi Shimon bar Yochai. Full of splendor was the revelation; hence, the wondrous book bears the title Zohar (Splendor)."
—A History of Jewish Literature, The Struggle of Mysticism By Israel Zinberg

The sudden appearance of the *Zohar* came at the hands of Moses De Leon (1250-1305), a rabbi and kabbalist living in Spain, who in about 1290 published and disseminated *Zoharic* booklets prepared from long-hidden original *Zohar* manuscripts. The *Zohar's* appearance in Spain ignited a flurry of controversy and renewed interest in mystical pursuits. Those who opposed the *Zohar* claimed it was a forgery, produced by De Leon for the sole purpose of profiting from its sales. On the other hand, kabbalists who grasped the secrets of the *Zohar* were unanimous in their conviction that only someone of the stature of Rabbi Shimon could produce such a magnificent work of enlightenment and power.

The emergence of the *Zohar* ultimately became the impetus for the proliferation of kabbalistic study over the next seven centuries. To study the *Zohar* is to study the deepest secrets of Kabbalah, the two—*Zohar* and Kabbalah—being synonymous.

THE CONTROVERSY

The controversy that swirled around the true origins of the *Zohar*, also known as the "*Midrash of Rav Shimon bar Yochai*," was not easily put to rest. The noted astronomer and rabbinical scholar Rabbi Abraham Zacuto (1450-1510) was of the opinion that the teachings of the *Zohar* are unquestionably those of Rabbi Shimon, transcribed by his disciples over time, in a manner similar to the redaction of the Talmud. This view is supported by kabbalists who claim that Rabbi Abba, the scribe of Rabbi Shimon, wrote the *Zohar* under the instruction of his master; for Rabbi Abba possessed a gift for writing in the poetic, veiled language of parable and metaphor. Therefore, he was uniquely equipped to both express the *Zohar*'s wisdom and to limit it to those who could understand the holy verses.

In his book *The Wisdom of the Zohar – an Anthology of Texts, Volume One*, scholar Isaiah Tishby points out that Rabbi Avraham Zacuto's *Sefer Yuhasin* (*Book of Geneologies*) contains "*a single fragmentary piece of evidence*" concerning the origins of the *Zohar*. This evidence comes in the form of testimony by the Kabbalist Rabbi Isaac of Acre, who was so moved by the heavenly power of the *Zohar's* text that he traveled to Toledo to inquire about its origins. Rabbi Isaac said that the Hebrew sections of the *Zohar* were forged and that the Aramaic verses were from the hand of Rabbi Shimon bar Yochai. Rabbi Isaac also reported hearing many different stories from many different scholars. Some said the book arrived from the Holy Land through the efforts of Nachmanides and his son. Others told Rabbi Isaac that Moses De Leon wrote the book himself through the power of the Divine Name, and that he ascribed it to Rabbi Shimon in order to profit handsomely from this work.

During his travels, Rabbi Isaac met De Leon himself, who swore that he possessed the original manuscript. Before he could show it to Rabbi Isaac, De Leon died, adding further intrigue to the case. One story given to Rabbi Isaac third-hand claimed that De Leon's wife and daughter alleged that De Leon had forged it in order to make a living. Another source, Rabbi Joseph Halevi said, "*Take it for a fact that the Zohar that Rabbi Shimon bar Yochai wrote was in possession of Rabbi Moses, and he [Rabbi Moses] copied from it and gave the copies to whoever he wished."*

It turns out that Rabbi Halevi tested De Leon. He claimed that he lost his copy of the manuscript and asked De Leon to write him a new one. The second version was identical to the first, right down to every minute detail, according to Rabbi Halevi. However, this test was still not accepted by others as proof. Perhaps De Leon made one complete forged copy and all other copies were made from the original forgery.

Rabbi Isaac then met Rabbi Jacob, a beloved student of Rabbi Moses De Leon, who claimed to know the full story. But for some reason, the portion of Rabbi Isaac's book that recounts Rabbi Jacob's testimony suddenly stops in mid-sentence.

According to the eighteenth-century Kabbalist Rabbi Hayim Joseph David Azulai (the Chidah 1724-1807) in his manuscript, *Shem haGedolim*, there is yet another version of the origins of the *Zohar*, which concerns a king who ordered an excavation in search of treasure but instead found the *Zohar*. It was brought to the wise men of Christendom, who failed to decipher it. So they brought the enigmatic manuscript to the hub of kabbalistic study, Toledo, Spain where it came into the hands of Moses De Leon.

This particular account comes closest to the oral version transmitted by the kabbalists. However, according to the oral transmission there are pieces missing from the original manuscript of Rabbi Azulai and from certain manuscripts of Rabbi Abraham Rovigo (1650-1713) and Rabbi Moses Zacuto (1625-1697); these missing fragments solve the puzzle of the origins of *Zohar*. The time is not yet right for the full revelation of this story, but it is my profoundest hope that the world will achieve the merit to see the publication of the full account speedily, in our day. For the revelation of any wisdom of *Zohar*, including its history, is in fact, the revelation of the *Or HaGanuz* (the Hidden Light).

For now, let us examine the view of the saintly 20th century Kabbalist Rav Yehuda Ashlag (1885-1954), who writes:

> *Those who are familiar with the Zohar, by which I mean whoever understands what is written in it, have all been unanimous in maintaining that its author was the godly Tanna, Rabbi Shimon bar Yochai, except for those who are far from this wisdom. Some of them have doubts on this point, and, on the basis of facts that were invented by those who opposed this wisdom, tend to maintain that the authorship of the*

Zohar is to be attributed to the Kabbalist Rabbi Moshe De Leon, or someone else of the same period.

As for myself, from the day that I have been enabled, by means of the Light of God, to peruse this holy book a little, it never entered my mind to investigate its authorship. The reason for this is simple. The contents of the book caused my mind to conjure up the cherished excellence of the Tanna Rabbi Shimon bar Yochai incalculably more than any of the other holy Tannaim [Rabbinical sages of the Mishnaic Period 70-200 CE] However, had it been absolutely clear to me that the author was someone else, Rabbi Moshe De Leon of blessed memory for example, then I would consider the excellence of Rabbi Moshe De Leon of blessed memory more than all the Tannaim, including Rabbi Shimon bar Yochai. However, because of the depth of the wisdom in the book, had I found clear proof that its author was one of the forty-eight prophets, this would have been more acceptable to me than to attribute it to one of the Tannaim. It would be even more acceptable to me had I proof that our teacher Moshe received it on Mount

Sinai from God, then my mind would be truly at rest; for this work is really fitting to be God's. However, since I have had the merit to compile a commentary that should prove adequate for whoever wishes to understand some of what is written in the book, I think I am hereby exempted from entering into an investigation on this subject. For no student of the Zohar could ever be satisfied with the possibility that its author could be of lesser rank than the Tanna, the holy Rabbi Shimon bar Yochai.

Dissemination of the Zohar

If the world's literature holds any volumes that might truly be designated as being complete, or, in the language of Kabbalah, as being "sealed with ten seals," that work is the *Zohar*.

After its appearance in Spain, the *Zohar* was soon recognized as the fundamental work of the Kabbalah, and therefore as the premier textbook of Jewish mysticism. However, because of the highly esoteric nature of its teachings, not to mention the difficulties presented by its original language, which was partly Aramaic and partly ancient Hebrew, the *Zohar* remained inaccessible for centuries to all but a few learned and carefully chosen initiates.

The *Zohar* manuscripts were written in the form of a commentary on the Bible, and contain several sections. The main section, *Sefer haZohar*, is related to the weekly story of the Bible. To this section the following are attached:

1. *Idra Rabba* (Greater Assembly), which was written when Rabbi Shimon and his son Rabbi Elazar emerged from the cave and selected eight disciples, who, together with Rabbi Shimon and his son, formed the "Greater Assembly." As mentioned previously, this is where the esoteric internal teachings of the Torah were revealed for the first time.

2. *Sifra diTzni'uta* (The Book of the Veiled Mystery), inserted before the Story of *Tetzaveh*, which deals with the structure of the creative process;

3. *Sitrei Torah* (Secrets of the Torah), which discusses the power of the Divine Names, and how they are used to tap the immense power of the cosmos;

4. *Idra Zuta* (The Small Assembly), which describes those teachings of Rabbi Shimon bar Yochai that were not revealed during the Greater Assembly but on the day of Rabbi Shimon's death;

5. *Ra'aya Mehemna* (Faithful Shepherd, or Moses), which deals with those cosmic precepts and doctrines not covered in the discourses between Elijah the Prophet and Rabbi Shimon bar Yochai;

6. *Midrash haNe'elam* (Recondite Exposition), which contains a vast collection of scriptural exposition concerning the methods of numerology, i.e. the permutations and combinations of the letters of the Hebrew alphabet and numerals;

7. *Zohar Hadash* (The New *Zohar*) is additional commentary to the Five Books of Moses along the same lines as the main body of the *Zohar*, and offers commentary, in addition to the Torah of The Song of Songs, and the Books of Ruth and *Eichah* (Lamentations);

8. *Tikunei Zohar* (Emendations of the *Zohar*), which addresses the same general subject matter as the *Zohar*, but is written as seventy two different commentaries on the first word of the Book of Genesis—*Beresheet. Tikunei Zohar* discourses upon teachings specifically directed to the Age of Aquarius;

9. *Hashmatot,* a volume of the *Zohar* that contains chapters and pages that for some reason were separated from the main body of the *Zohar* during the original publication. When those parts reappeared they were printed as an additional volume;

10. *Tosefta* (Additions), which adds some fragmentary supplements to the *Zohar* in which references to the *Sefirot* (the Emanations) are made.

According to the kabbalists, the *Zohar* is more than just a commentary on the Torah. As the *Zohar* itself declares,

> *"How beloved are the words of Torah that each and every word has lofty secrets*

and the entire Torah is considered supernal. We learned IN THE BARAITA of the thirteen qualities of the Torah. Whatever is part of the whole, yet it is an exception, it is so in order to teach a general rule, not teach merely about itself. Since the Torah is the highest generality, even though a simple story is an exception to the rule, its function most certainly is not merely to tell us just that story but rather to demonstrate the highest matters and the utmost secrets."
—*The Zohar, Beha'alotcha 3:13*

The truth of the matter is that every word of the Bible contains a sublime coded mystery which, when deciphered, reveals a wealth of elevated meaning. The narratives of the Torah are but outer garments in which the real meaning is clothed. This was precisely the idea to which King David addressed himself when he declared, *"Open my eyes that I might behold wondrous things from your Torah."* (Psalms 119:18) In essence, the Bible is considered to be an encoded cosmic message that the *Zohar* reveals by virtue of its various discourses and by its penetrating insights.

The Bible has long been viewed as a collection of morality tales. From the *Zoharic* perspective, the

Bible is not intended merely to improve the outward conduct of humankind but to assist each individual in creating an intimate personal relationship with the Light of the Creator that permeates every inch of the cosmos. In ancient times even the most mundane events of everyday life were associated with the Divine.

To the kabbalist, it was apparent that, in a very real and profound sense, humanity and the cosmos were inseparable. The kabbalists believed that mankind could raise its consciousness through the *Zohar* and transcend the crushing weight of earthly concerns. In the right hands, the *Zohar* would be a tool of immense power. It could, when properly understood, provide answers to humankind's most seemingly baffling problems.

According to the great Kabbalist Moshe Chaim Luzzatto, the revelation of the *Zohar's* secrets would be an ongoing process whereby each new generation of kabbalists would unravel more mysteries concealed within the *Zohar's* texts, thus revealing more of the Light and Energy that was lost on Mount Sinai as a consequence of the sin of the golden calf. To the kabbalist, it was merely a matter of time before a certain threshold of wisdom—and thus Light—would be revealed as a result of unleashing the mysteries of the *Zohar*. The darkness that permeates human existence would finally give way to a never-ending illumination of Light manifesting as the arrival of the Messiah and our Final Redemption. The *Zohar* promised that with the ushering in of the Messianic Era—the End of Days—the mysteries of the Universe and all existence will become fully accessible to human understanding, resulting in the complete removal of pain and suffering and death from our landscape.

After the expulsion of the Jews from Spain in 1492, the fountainhead of kabbalistic activity moved to the mystical town of Safed, located in Northern Israel amid the historic mountains of Galilee. This relocation of kabbalistic power took place as Christopher Columbus embarked upon his voyage of discovery in search of the Americas. Both events have a profound connection to the book called *Zohar*.

THE ZOHAR'S
INFLUENCE ON THE

RENAISSANCE,
THE AGE OF DISCOVERY
AND SCIENCE

CHRISTOPHER COLUMBUS
(1451–1506)

A crater on the moon, Zagut Crater, is named after Rabbi Abraham Zacuto, the previously noted 16th century astronomer, mathematician, historian and astrologer. Rabbi Zacuto studied at the University of Salamanca and eventually was assumed the chair of astronomy and mathematics. Rabbi Zacuto was also the Royal Astronomer to the Court of Portugal. He was responsible for replacing the inaccurate wooden astrolabe with one made of copper. His most famous book was the *Almanac Perpetuum*, an astronomical work and almanac which paved the way for the new age of exploration by Columbus and others.

Rabbi Zacuto was one of the few supporters of Columbus' goal to sail to the new world. The two men knew each other, and Rabbi Zacuto's Tables accompanied Columbus on all his voyages. In an age when the scientific, political, and religious communities feared the dangers of sailing a ship over the edge of a flat Earth, Columbus and Rabbi Zacuto were certain the world was indeed a sphere.

Dr. Harry Gershenowitz, professor emeritus of Biological Sciences at Glassboro State College when interviewed said:

"It was the Zohar, 100 percent, that influenced both Rabbi Zacuto and Columbus in regards to a spherical Earth. It was the Zohar that provided knowledge of a round Earth and the idea of there being many geographical continents, thus giving credence to Columbus' endeavor."

The ancient *Zohar* text put it this way:

"The Earth revolves in a circle, as a ball. Some [people] are above and some below. And all the inhabitants [humans] have different appearances. The different appearances of the inhabited world are directly dependent upon the difference of the cosmic air and force that exists in seven major geographical locations. And because of this, there is a location on the globe where it is light to some inhabitants while it is dark to others. This creates day on one side and night on the other. There is a location where the day is very long, almost always light, and the night is very short. This account of the universal structure and the seven different cosmic atmospheres is to be found in the book of the ancients and in the Book of Adam. This mystery has been entrusted to the masters of the Kabbalah,

> *but it is not known to those who mark out boundaries—the geographers—because it is a very deep secret in the Torah [the Bible]."*

Why has the influence of the *Zohar* on Columbus remained in the dark for so long? Dr. Gershenowitz explains it in the following way:

> *"The Western World could not accept these truths in regards to Columbus, the Zohar, and the role of the Sephardic Jews in the discovery of America because the Christian world did not accept the Hebrew faith—spiritually and geographically. They were wrong in their story of Columbus but they outnumbered the Sephardic Jews and so their version of the story prevailed."*

RABBI ISAAC LURIA
(THE ARI OR HOLY LION—1534-1572)

Without question, Kabbalist Rabbi Isaac Luria (the Ari) is one of the most influential and revered Kabbalists of all time. Safed was the home of the Ari during his most active years of teaching the *Zohar* to his students, who were known as the Lion Cubs.

Safed was home to a number of other great kabbalists as well: Joseph Caro (1488-1575), author of the *Shulchan Aruch*, the profound codification and compilation of the Laws of Torah; Rabbi Moses Cordovero (1522-1570), once a teacher of the Ari; Rabbi Solomon Alkabetz (1500-1580), who composed the famous Sabbath Hymn *Lecha Dodi*, which was sung by the Ari and his disciples to welcome in the Sabbath; and Rabbi Chaim Vital (1543-1620), the Ari's most important student.

The Ari would walk the hills of Galilee with his students and instruct them in the deepest mysteries of the *Zohar*. As noted earlier, the poetic language of the *Zohar*, and its use of metaphor and parable, concealed its mysteries from the unworthy. Until the Ari, the esoteric nature of the *Zohar* was incomprehensible to the average student. The Ari literally decoded the *Zohar* through his famous discourses; it was left to his disciple, Rabbi Chaim Vital, and his son, Rabbi Shmuel Vital, to commit the Ari's oral teachings to writing, thus giving birth to what is now known as Lurianic Kabbalah.

The *Zohar* and Lurianic Kabbalah had an immediate and profound impact upon the Renaissance, most particularly on the scientific thinkers who brought about what became known as the Scientific Revolution. This may explain why the Ari's insights into the origins of the physical Universe bear such a striking resemblance to modern day science, specifically the Big Bang Theory, which postulates the initial event that gave birth to the Universe, and superstring theory, which attempts to reconcile the microcosmic subatomic realm of quantum physics with the macrocosmic realm of classical physics. The congruencies between the *Zohar*—as seen through the lens of Lurianic Kabbalah—and contemporary physics have been noted by various scientists and scholars. The *Zohar* and Lurianic Kabbalah had an immediate and profound impact upon the Renaissance, most particularly the scientific minds that brought about what became known as the Scientific Revolution.

PARACELSUS
(1493-1541)

Pharmaceutical companies such as Pfizer and Johnson and Johnson owe their existence to a Swiss scientist and alchemist who lived in the 16th century and is known and recognized as the father of modern medicine and the father of toxicology. His name was Auroleus Phillipus Theostratus Bombastus von Hohenheim and he literally created the field of pharmacology. His full name was quite a mouthful and thus he became better known as Paracelsus.

Paracelsus, one of the most brilliant physicians, scientists and alchemists of the Renaissance, introduced the use of chemicals and minerals into the practice of medicine.

According to Encyclopedia Britannica Paracelsus "established the role of chemistry in medicine." Paracelsus was also the mentor of the illustrious chemist Jan Baptista van Helmont, who discovered and thus introduced the word *gas* into the lexicon of science.

The *United States National Library of Medicine* credits Paracelsus for helping to bring about the medical revolution of the Renaissance and the birth of the modern world. According to an Exhibition put on by the United States Government and the National Institute of Health celebrating the 500 year anniversary of the birth of Paracelsus:

> *"By the mid-seventeenth century there had been almost a century of debate, but many of the medical views of Paracelsus were to prevail in the end. The academic acceptance of chemistry by physicians surely was one of the chief accomplishments of his school. Beyond this, the significance of his opening of medical thought to this new approach can be compared with that of the*

influence of Copernicus on astronomy and physics during the same period."

Paracelsus asserts in one of his written works:

"All of you . . . who see land beyond the horizon, who read sealed, hidden missives and books, who seek for buried treasures in the earth and in walls, you who teach so much wisdom, such high arts—remember that you must take unto yourselves the teachings of the Kabbalah if you want to accomplish all this. For the Kabbalah builds on a true foundation."

—Jolanda Jacobi, ed., *Paracelsus: Selected Writings* (Princeton, NJ: Princeton University Press, 1979)

Paracelsus credits the ancient teachings of Kabbalah as the foundation of his and all knowledge.

DR. JOHN DEE
(1527-1608)

John Dee was unquestionably one of the most brilliant minds during the age of Queen Elizabeth l. Dee was proficient in a number of disciplines, universally recognized as a renowned mathematician, geographer, astronomer, astrologer, scientist, and personal adviser to Queen Elizabeth. Internationally famous for his genius, Dee was the first person to utilize Euclidean geometry for navigation.

John Dee, the official Royal Astrologer advising Queen Elizabeth 1, also chose Elizabeth's coronation date based on his knowledge of astrology.

In a conversation with Dr. Matt Goldish, professor of Judaic History, Ohio State University, he explained the importance of Dee and his connection to Kabbalah:

> *"John Dee was considered to be the most learned man in Elizabethan England. He was living in the time of Queen Elizabeth and Shakespeare. There were quite a number of very smart people doing some very important work as it was early on in the scientific revolution and it was the period of the voyages of exploration. Yet John Dee was considered the most learned of them all. He was extremely influential in the development of mathematical ideas. John Dee was heavily influenced by the Kabbalah. There is no doubt about it. He uses Kabbalah in his Monas Hiergoglyphica,*

his great work in which he brings
together all the secrets of the Universe. "

As the noted British historian Frances Yates writes:

"Dee was, in his own right, a brilliant
mathematician, and he related his study
of numbers to the three worlds of the
Kabbalists. In the lower elemental world
he studied number as technology and
applied science and his Preface to Euclid
provided a brilliant survey of the
mathematical arts in general. "

— *The Rosicrucian Enlightenment: Francis Yates*
  Selected Works, 1999

When speaking with Deborah Harkness,
Professor of History at the University of Southern
California, she said that Dee was a serious student
of Kabbalah:

"John Dee was probably the most
important and influential natural
philosopher and scientist, living and
working in England in the 16th century.
John Dee was the Kabbalist at Queen
Elizabeth's court as well as being her
personal astrologer, a mathematician
and a navigational expert. John Dee
was enormously influenced by

Kabbalah. He had an extensive Kabbalistic library. The best one in England hands down in the 16th century. It was Kabbalah that drove all of his work."

According to Harkness, Dee was convinced that Kabbalah could reveal the hidden truth about the natural world through hidden messages that God embedded into this physical reality. He looked to Kabbalah as the singular way to reconcile and unite all the physical laws of the natural world with the spiritual laws that govern the metaphysical reality. Kabbalah, according to John Dee could unify and harmonize the world and present a complete picture of human existence.

THE ROME CONNECTION

The Talmud tells us that Rabbi Shimon, the author of the *Zohar*, visited Rome during his lifetime. When the Roman Emperor Marcus Aurelius's daughter fell ill the great Kabbalist healed her and, in turn, Aurelius annulled a set of decrees issued against the Israelites by Rome.

The influence of the *Zohar*, Rabbi Shimon and the emergence of Kabbalah in the middle ages can be seen to this very day in a most historical setting.

In the book, *The Sistine Secrets, Michelangelo's Forbidden Messages in the Heart of the Vatican, by Benjamin Blech and Roy Doliner,* we learn that many Kabbalistic symbols are integrated into the designs of the smallest and most famous city on Earth—Vatican City; specifically, the Sistine Chapel.

According to the authors, Michelangelo was likely exposed to Kabbalah while living in Florence where interest in Kabbalah flourished around a Platonic Academy founded by the Medici Family of Florence. Michelangelo lived with and was supported by the famous Medici family. Lorenzo Medici literally controlled the city and gathered together great minds and great artists, many of whom studied the *Zohar*, to help enrich Florence. Using the lens of Kabbalah to decipher Michelangelo's work in the Sistine Chapel, the authors of the book found profound connections to the wisdom of the *Zohar*. For instance, when painting the Tree of Knowledge of Good and Evil, the famed Florentine artist depicted it as a fig tree as opposed to the traditional apple tree. The concept of the fig tree being connected to the Tree of Knowledge would only be known to someone familiar with the Talmud and the *Zohar*, as both connect the Tree of Knowledge to the fruit of the fig.

Michelangelo's painting of the prophet Jonah features the ancient sage with bare legs in the shape of the Hebrew letter *Hei*. A major component of Kabbalah is *gematria*, the study of the numerical values of Hebrew letters and words in order to glean additional insights from biblical texts. The numerical value of the letter *Hei* is five. Remarkably, Michelangelo included two angels in the painting (though there are no angels in this particular biblical story), one of which has a hand opened wide displaying five fingers. This alludes to the letter *Hei* just below the angel. As the authors state:

> *"The upper angel is holding up his outspread fingers, showing us the number five. The lower angel is looking directly at Jonah's bare legs, as if to say 'Look for five down below."*

Symbols such as the Shield of David (a true kabbalistic cipher) and the kabbalistic Tree of Life or Ten *Sefirot* appear on the floor of the Sistine Chapel. The Pope actually kneels down on the Ten *Sefirot*, which the authors suggest is really a "Kabbalistic meditational device."

As *The Sistine Secrets* point out, Michelangelo brilliantly sabotaged the original plan for the Sistine Chapel. Pope Julius II wanted the chapel to reflect the power and grand achievements of the papal family. The objective was to showcase the leading figures of Christianity including Jesus, the Virgin Mary, and the apostles.

Michelangelo had other ideas. According to *The Sistine Secrets*, "Michelangelo was able to subvert the entire project in order to secretly promote his own ideals." The famed genius "was able to paint the largest fresco in the Catholic world without even a single Christian figure in it—only figures from the Hebrew Bible."

The book further explains, "It is also significant that the Sistine frescoes are not only faithful to the Hebrew Bible, but even more so to the Kabbalah...."

THE CHRISTIAN KABBALISTS

The preeminent Christian scholars, philosophers, and scientists during the Renaissance and the age of Scientific Revolution were all avid students of Kabbalah. They believed with great conviction that Kabbalah held within it the true secrets of the Christian faith, including the original teachings of Jesus. One of these prominent Christian scholars was Count Giovanni Pico della Mirandola of Florence (1463-1494). He is generally credited with injecting the mystical teachings of kabbalistic wisdom into the very nucleus of the Italian Renaissance, planting a seed that would blossom into what became a sudden eruption of scientific advancement and discovery.

Johannes Reuchlin (1455-1522), a brilliant German scholar, one of the country's greatest, met Pico while traveling to Italy as young man. Pico and other Christian Kabbalists piqued Reuchlin's interest in Kabbalah. Reuchlin delved into kabbalistic study with great fervor, producing written works in which he credited Kabbalah as the prime influence and source of wisdom for the great minds of history, including Pythagoras. He believed that all Christians should learn Aramaic and Hebrew so that they could study the *Zohar*, and other great kabbalistic texts.

Both Pico and Reuchlin were convinced that Kabbalah authenticated the major tenets of Christianity. They believed Kabbalah embodied the essence of Christianity and all religions.

Moreover, as mentioned previously, the Light of the *Zohar* dates back to Moses and Mount Sinai where it was referred to as the *Or HaGanuz* (Hidden Light), that was snuffed out when the first Tablets were broken. Moses then entered a cave on Sinai where he received a second set of Tablets, which caused Moses' face to shine. Medieval Kabbalist and astronomer

Rabbi Abraham Ibn Ezra (1093-1167) points out that Moses' face radiated after receiving the Second Tablets, a phenomenon that did not occur with the first tablets. Moreover, Rabbi Ibn Ezra utilizes the word *Zohar* to describe the Light on Moses' face.

Rabbi Levi Ben Gershom (Gersonides 1288-1344) confirms Rabbi Ibn Ezra's remarkable insight. Gersonides designates the illumination on Moses face as *Zohar*. So, too, does Rabbi Don Isaac Abarbanel (1437-1508), who further mentions that the word *Zohar*, being used for the purpose of describing the luminosity of Moses' face, connects to a very deep secret. Finally, Rabbi Shlomo Yitzhaki (Rashi 1040-1105), famed as the author of the first comprehensive commentaries on the Torah, points out that the word used in the Torah to describe the veil that conceals this beaming *Zoharic* radiance of Moses countenance is actually an Aramaic word (*masveh*)—not Hebrew. Here we have an Aramaic veil concealing a Divine Light that is referred to as *Zohar*, a precise parallel itself to the Aramaic book called *Zohar*. Rabbi Ibn Ezra also explains that the heavenly realm, the source of all Divine Radiance, is structured as a book.

This reinforces the kabbalistic thought that the *Zohar* is none other than the *Or HaGanuz* (the Hidden Light) that was lost when the first Tablets shattered and the second Tablets (along with the remnants of the first) were hidden away in the Ark of the Covenant. This also positions the Book of Splendor as the true inner teaching and embodiment of both Torah and Christianity. According to the eminent Kabbalist Rav Moses David Valle (d. 1777), disciple and colleague of Rav Moshe Chaim Luzzatto, both Jews and Christians have long failed to understand their own kabbalistic roots and identity. This is an interesting observation considering that Rabbi Valle was viewed as the Messiah of his generation.

From the viewpoint of the kabbalists, we now have a "Messiah" informing both Jews and Christians that Kabbalah is not merely a spiritual branch or mystical interpretation of Torah; nor is it just a validation of Christianity. Rather, the *Zohar* is the source, the basis, the quintessence and ultimate truth of both Torah and Christianity. It was Kabbalah that was bestowed upon Moses at Sinai, the Torah being its material body, the *Zohar* its true essence and soul. The Ten Commandments (Ten Utterances) were simply a metaphor for the Ten *Sefirot* of *Keter, Chochmah, Binah, Chesed, Gevurah, Tiferet, Netzach, Hod, Yesod* and *Malchut,* with Moses holding the Tablets personifying the unification of *Zeir Anpin* (*Chesed, Gevurah, Tiferet, Netzach, Hod and Yesod*) and *Malchut,* the physical reality with the Divine Realm. It was through the sacred essence of kabbalistic technology that Moses was able to achieve this unification on Sinai, and it would be Kabbalah, through the heavenly book known as the *Zohar*, that would eventually be responsible for reigniting the Revelation of the Light at the End of Days.

When Pico, Reuchlin (and others we'll soon learn about) claimed that Kabbalah could reconcile all the faiths of the world and bring universal harmony, they were, in fact, echoing the teachings of the *Zohar* and the great kabbalists of history. These profound, deeply subtle truths were sensed by the great thinkers of the Renaissance when they entered the inner sanctum of kabbalistic study; the *Zohar* electrified many of the brightest Christian minds (while also alarming many religious authorities).

THE LATIN TRANSLATION OF ZOHAR: KABBALAH DENUDATA

Knorr von Rosenroth was a noted 17th century Christian alchemist, scholar, and advisor to German Prince Christian August. Knorr von Rosenroth, who was deeply immersed in Kabbalah, translated the *Zohar* and the writings of Kabbalist Isaac Luria into Latin, producing *Kabbalah Denudata* (Kabbalah Unveiled) in

1684. Like Pico and Reuchlin, von Rosenroth considered Kabbalah to be the true ancient wisdom given to Moses on Mount Sinai.

As scholar Allison Coudert points out in her book, *The Impact of Kabblah in the Seventeenth Century*, Knorr von Rosenroth believed Kabbalah: *"...offered nothing less than a blueprint of utopia. He was convinced that the Zohar provided answers to all the most perplexing questions...."*

Knorr was also certain the *Zohar* could help restore religious harmony, including the friction between Catholics and Protestants. Knorr blamed Christianity's underlying connection to pagan and Greek philosophy for its problems. He wrote,

> *"As often as I lamented that detestable discord within the Church it is possible to show that these evils have arisen chiefly from the begetter of dissension, our pagan philosophy."*

The Greeks, according to Knorr, derived their wisdom from the pure kabbalalistic truths of Torah but they corrupted and misrepresented them. By returning to the Kabbalah, the source of Christianity, in its true form, Christians could reunite in one faith.

Coudert puts it this way:

> *"Because the subject matter of the Kabbalah Denudata appears so esoteric, it has never been appreciated as a significant text for understanding the emergence of modern thought. But within this work one can find the basis for the faith in science, belief in progress, and commitment to religious toleration characteristic of the best aspects of western culture."*

Knorr's *Kabbalah Denudata* eventually made its way into the personal libraries of the greatest thinkers of the scientific revolution, significantly influencing a generation of philosophers and physicists in ways that are still not yet fully appreciated or understood.

BIRTH OF THE SCIENTIFIC REVOLUTION

The 17th century experienced an abrupt explosion of scientific advancement.

Concerning this impromptu eruption of scientific knowledge, scholar A.C. Crombie states in his book, *Medieval and Early Modern Science:*

"One outstanding fact about the Scientific Revolution is that its initial and in a sense most important stages were carried through before the invention of the new measuring instruments, the telescope, and microscope, thermometer and accurate clock, which were later to become indispensable for getting accurate and scientific answers to the questions that were to come to the forefront of science. In its initial states, in fact, the Scientific Revolution came about rather by a systematic change in intellectual outlook, in the type of questions asked, than by an increase in technical equipment. Why such a revolution in methods of thought should have taken place is obscure."

Scholars and scientists alike have been hard pressed to find a reason for this sudden revolution. Something must have sparked this rebirth of Western philosophy and science after the long dormancy of the Middle Ages, but what? Some scholars argue that it was Kabbalah that sparked the revolution in science, for the *Zohar* had a profound influence on many of the greatest scientists and mathematicians of the 16th and 17th centuries—a time when the lines between philosophy and science, physics and metaphysics, were virtually non-existent.

In the year 1559, thanks to the invention of the printing press, the *Zohar* was printed for the very first time. Ironically, it was the Catholic Church that contributed to the broad circulation of the *Zohar* and kabbalistic wisdom. At a time when the Roman Inquisition and the destruction of Jewish books were taking place, Pope Paul IV (1476-1559) himself gave his approval to the publication of the *Zohar*, which rolled off the printing presses.

The Kabbalist Isaac De Lattes, who was instrumental in the printing of the *Zohar*, offered a characteristically optimistic reason for the Church's approval of the printing of this preeminent body of Kabbalistic wisdom. In the first edition of the *Zohar*, printed in the city of Mantua, Isaac De Lattes wrote:

> *"That the hand of the government which rules over us with great wisdom has not harmed us the Kabbalists is to be explained only by the fact that the government has the good intention of removing the thorns and harsh expressions that provoke hatred between Christians and Jews."*

As a result of the printing of the *Zohar*, Kabbalah began to broaden its influence in profound ways. When addressing the question of what could have prompted the sudden eruption of philosophical and scientific advancement and discovery in the 17th century, scholar Max I. Dimont, in his book *Jews, God and History*, considered the role of the *Zohar* as a possible catalyst.

> *"A fifteen hundred-year philosophical and scientific dark age lies between Epictetus and Marcus Aurelius on the one hand and Bacon, Descartes, Locke, Leibniz, Copernicus, Kepler, Galileo, and Newton on the other... Did, perhaps, the Kabbalistic metaphysical speculations of such Jewish and Christian scholars... have something to do with laying the intellectual foundations for the seventeenth-century rebirth of philosophy and the establishment of scientific methodology in Western Europe?"*

In 1962, when Dimont wrote his book, evidence pointing to a kabbalistic connection with the likes of Sir Isaac Newton, Wilhelm Leibniz, and others had not yet emerged. Nonetheless Dimont suggested it might very well be the *Zohar* that had helped to ignite the unprecedented revolution in science.

Dimont points out that it was no coincidence that the surprising outbreak of Christian scientific thought did not actually occur in the centuries preceding the scientific revolution, or in Eastern Europe; rather, he explains, *"it took place in the seventeenth century, in Western Europe, in the area where Jewish kabbalists and scientists had flourished for four hundred years."* Dimont considered the kabbalists to be men of science, not just religious or spiritual adepts, and thus he believed that their works should be considered when examining the causes behind the scientific revolution. Dimont argues his point as follows:

> *"Because their works have been overshadowed by later non-Jewish scientists such as Galileo and Newton, I see no reason why the contributions of these early Jewish scientists should not be assessed. New ideas do not spring up in a vacuum. They bloom only in well-prepared intellectual soil."*

More than forty years ago Dimont said that Copernicus, Kepler, Galileo, Descartes, and the two greatest scientists of the renaissance, Leibniz and Newton, could very well have had access to the writings of the kabbalists. Recent scholarship supports Dimont's theories that Kabbalah and the *Zohar* influenced the greatest intellects of the

Renaissance, providing the spark for the greatest intellectual flowering in human history.

GOTTFRIED WILHELM LEIBNIZ
(1646-1716)

Seventeenth century German scientist Gottfried Leibniz, a renowned mathematician, physicist and philosopher, invented calculus about the same time as Isaac Newton. The two were at odds with each other, both arguing over who invented calculus first. Yet the contributions of Leibniz are not in doubt. As a result of discovering the binary number system, as well as designing one of the first calculating machines, he is considered to be the father of the modern day computer; and along with Newton, Leibniz is regarded as one of the greatest scientists in history.

Leibniz, first working on calculus in the 1770s, with some of his contributions in calculus still known as *Leibniz's Law*, was clearly ahead of his time. He foreshadowed Einstein by more than two centuries when he argued correctly, against Newton, that time, space and motion should be considered from a relativistic point of view. Newton considered them to be absolute. Leibniz's came extremely close to conceiving an early version of Quantum Theory, centuries before modern physics.

Leibniz, along with Descartes and Spinoza, was viewed as one of the great rationalists of the seventeenth century. Throughout history, scholars and scientists biased against mysticism have tried to portray Leibniz as a rationalist with no interest in mystical or spiritual matters, most especially Kabbalah. To this day there is no complete edition of Leibniz's writings, and it is well known that many of his papers have yet to be published; however, important information on Leibniz keeps cropping up. Allison Coudert, Professor of Religious Studies at the University of California, Davis, investigated a cache of untouched Leibniz documents at the Leibniz archives in Hanover, northern Germany, and found the influence of a man named Francis Mercury van Helmont, renowned for his expertise in Kabbalah. As Coudert pointed out,

> *"van Helmont edited the Kabbalah Denudata (the Latin translation of the Zohar) and everywhere he went, Kabbalah went with him."*

Coudert discovered that van Helmont introduced Leibniz to Kabbalah, which profoundly influenced Leibniz's philosophy and views concerning the nature of reality and the structure of the cosmos. Matter and spirit, according to Leibniz, were merely two opposite ends of one continuum, an idea congruent with *Zoharic* and Lurianic teachings that spirit, energy, or Light thickens relative to its distance from the non-material Cause of all Causes known as the *Ein Sof,* or the Endless World.

Moreover, Leibniz, like van Helmont and Knorr von Rosenroth, believed that Kabbalah, called *prisca theologia,* personified an ancient secret wisdom that God had secretly revealed to Moses on Mount Sinai. Leibniz believed that if this pure wisdom was rediscovered and revealed to the world in its original, uncorrupted form it would bring about world peace by establishing a foundation for a true universal spirituality, putting an end to the religious conflicts that have left the landscape of human civilization soaked in blood. Leibniz very much wanted to unite Catholics and Protestants, Christians, Muslims and Jews, and he believed Kabbalah was the means to achieve this end.

SIR ISAAC NEWTON
(1643-1727)

Newton's heirs, along with various scholars and scientists over the centuries, went to great lengths to portray Newton as an atheistic, rational man of science who offered up a mechanistic view of the Universe without any need of a Divine

Source to oversee the operation of the cosmos. Newton's universe, according to this portrait, was like a giant clock lacking soul and spirit, an enormous mechanism which was merely the sum total of its moving parts. This was hardly the case. The truth about Newton's mystical and kabbalistic pursuits were buried along with Newton upon his death. His family decided to keep his theological/mystical writings sealed for several hundred years, until finances became a problem.

After Newton's death, all of his theological manuscripts were kept private by his niece, Katherine Conduitt, who feared their public release would besmirch her uncle's reputation. And although a genius like Sir Isaac Newton understood that spiritual wisdom and physics were two sides of one coin, many rejected this holistic approach to nature and the mysteries of the Universe. Theology and mysticism were out. Materialism and atheism were in. In the late 1800s, it was no longer politically correct to commingle spirituality and science. However, in 1935, Newton's theological manuscripts, including his copy of the *Zohar*, were finally auctioned off at Sotheby's. To the chagrin of many scholars and scientists, this brought about a surge of awareness of Newton's mystical interests that transformed the world's view of Newton; and there was no turning back.

Albert Einstein was given access to Newton's mystical writings, and in a letter dated September 1940, Einstein wrote:

> *"I take great interest in Newton's writings on biblical subject matters, since they provide me with a deep insight into his spiritual makeup and the way this important person works. Newton firmly believes in the Bible being derived from Divine Inspiration..... He (Newton) is firmly convinced that the seemingly dark sections in the Bible hold great revelations, and one has to simply strive to decipher the underlying symbolic language. Newton approaches this process of deciphering or interpretation by way of sharp, systematic thinking and by carefully studying various available sources."*
> *—September 1940, Lake Saranac*

Those sources include the *Zohar*. To the surprise of scholars, Newton owned his own personal copy of the *Zohar*, the *Kabbalah Denudata*, or Latin version. Newton's *Zohar* is still archived at Trinity College in Cambridge.

Physicist Dr. Michio Kaku is an internationally recognized authority in theoretical physics and a best selling author. Kaku says that Newton *"kept a lot of these beliefs secret, not because he wanted to, but because he'd have been fired if his real beliefs came out."* In fact, Newton ended up writing more about Kabbalah and mysticism than he did about science.

The eminent economist and scholar John Maynard Keynes confirmed the mystical portrait of Newton. Keynes said of Sir Isaac:

> *"Newton saw the whole Universe and all that is in it as a riddle, as a secret which could be read by applying pure thought to certain evidence—certain mystic clues which God had hid about the world to allow a sort of philosopher's treasure hunt to the esoteric brotherhood. He believed that these clues were to be found partly in the evidence of the heavens and in the constitution of elements, but also partly in certain papers and traditions handed down by the brethren in an unbroken chain back to the original cryptic revelation."*

Newton's view of the Bible as a cosmic code or cryptogram was congruent with the views of the Kabbalists throughout history. It's worth noting that Newton went to the trouble of learning the Hebrew language so that he could extract these great Kabbalistic secrets from the scriptures.

Scholar George Zollschan in his paper, *God's Sensorium: Newton's Kabbalistic Slip*, states that Newton's famous description of space as *sensorium dei* is the result of Kabbalistic influence. *Sensorium dei* means God causes Creation and movement by "perceiving" rather than by willing or speaking. This notion, Zollschan asserts, has only one precedent: The Kabbalistic teachings of 16th century Kabbalist Isaac Luria. Second, Newton sees space as existing within God, the *sensorium dei*, which Zollschan points out is similar to the kabbalistic concept known as *makom pannui* (empty space) and vacuum God created when He withdrew an aspect of His Energy and Light.

Perhaps the most telling *Zoharic* influence upon Sir Isaac can be seen in one of Newton's greatest experiments and discoveries. Newton shone a light through a prism and discovered that white light contains all the colors of the spectrum. Newton's personal copy of the *Zohar* describes the exact same idea when discussing the mechanics of both physical and spiritual Light:

> *"...colors blend with each other ...except for the white color in which all are incorporated..."*
> — *Zohar Vol. 22 37:140*

The Ancients

Interestingly, the way in which contemporary scholars and scientists now confirm the impact that Kabbalah had upon the scientific minds of the Renaissance, is very similar to the way the great thinkers of that time viewed the intellects of ancient history and their connection to Kabbalistic wisdom.

Newton, in his own handwritten manuscript, stated that Plato derived all of his most important ideas from Kabbalah:

> *"Plato traveling to Egypt when the Jews were numerous in that country learnt there his metaphysical opinions about the superior beings and formal causes of all things, which he calls Ideas and which the kabbalists call Sefirot."*
> —*Sir Isaac Newton (MS. Yehuda, 15.7, p. 137v)*

Nor was this Kabbalistic connection limited to Plato. In fact, the list of those classical luminaries who reportedly derived their ideas from Kabbalah reads like a Who's Who of ancient Greece. For instance, Pythagoras (569– 475 BCE) is considered one of the world's greatest thinkers. He was a philosopher and the world's first pure mathematician. He and his followers devised the famous *Pythagorean Theorem*. He excelled in math, astronomy, and music. Pythagoras contributed to the musical theory specifically relating to the connection between math and music, pitch, the twelve tones, and natural properties of sound. According to Hermippus of Smyrna, the 3rd century philosopher, Pythagoras owed all of his theories to the Jews. He accused Pythagoras of imitating the doctrines of the Jews and transferring them into his own philosophy.

Yosef Ben Matityahu, better known as Titus Flavious Josephus, was a historian in the 1st century CE. More widely read in Europe than any other author, he provided priceless eye-witness accounts of this significant period of western religion. Josephus said that it is *"truly affirmed of Pythagoras that he took a great many of the laws of the Jews into his own philosophy."*

RABBI
MOSHE CHAIM LUZZATTO
(RAMCHAL 1707-1746)

He has been called the most brilliant thinker of the last few hundred years. Rabbi Moshe Chaim Luzzatto—known by the acronym *Ramchal*—was born in Padua, Italy, and at a young age he led a mystical circle in the study of *Zohar* that literally operated on a twenty-four-hour basis.

Rabbi Luzzatto was a disciple of Lurianic Kabbalah, and with help of a *maggid* (a heavenly being in charge of the highest wisdom), he revealed wondrous new insights into Kabbalah and the *Zohar* with the intent to bring about the Final Redemption.

Rabbi Luzzatto said that the time of Rabbi Shimon bar Yochai was one of great darkness, hence the destruction of the Temple and slaughtering of so many Israelites. The Ramchal taught that Rabbi Shimon's revelation of the *Zohar* was a cosmic infusion into the physical reality emanating from the *Sefirotic* dimension known as *Yesod.* The revelation of the *Zohar* prevented the destruction of the world and served to maintain its existence until the actual Final Redemption but, according to the Ramchal, it was a tiny moment of illumination in relation to the Light that would be needed for the ultimate Redemption.

The Ramchal saw himself and his mystic circle as heirs to and emulators of the kabbalistic circles of Ari and Rabbi Shimon's circle in the *Idra Rabba.* In a larger context, Rabbi Luzzatto, and his disciple and colleague Rav Moses David Valle felt that their task was to complete the revelation of the *Zohar* in the world, thereby ending the scourge of pain, suffering, and even death itself.

The Ramchal went to work on what is known as a Second *Zohar* (*Zohar Tinyana*), a deeper, more insightful work designed to reveal additional *Zoharic* secrets and thus infuse greater spiritual Light into the world in order to hasten the Messianic era. In 1931, scholar Simon Ginzburg wrote a biography of the Ramchal in which he describes Luzzatto's efforts at writing the Second *Zohar*. States Ginzburg: *"He was at that time a fountain of energy inexhaustible, almost superhuman."*

Unfortunately, Luzzatto's mystic practices and lofty Messianic goals agitated many rabbis of his day, most notably Rabbi Moses Hagiz (1671-1750). As Ginzburg reports, Hagiz threatened to inform the Kaiser and the Pope of Rabbi Luzzatto's activities so that the Ramchal would wind up burned at the stake for heresy. Consequently many of the Ramchal's kabbalistic writings, including the Second *Zohar*, were either buried or burned, thus delaying the transformation of the world.

In response to the controversy surrounding the Ramchal, his teacher, the esteemed and renowned Talmudic master Rabbi Isaiah Bassan, wrote:

> *"As to the man of valor against whom all this noise is directed, I will say just a few lines, not too many. Because I am like him, as I was to him like a father.*

But the truth should be stated, that while a young child, he came to love the Torah with an affectionate love, and when he grew into boyhood, he made for himself a golden coat of modesty, without following things of vanity and the impulses of his heart, the foolish impulses of childhood and boyhood. God gave him sense to listen and to understand and he was to me like a son. I trained him, I took him into my arms, I taught him as much as I know, and as I loved him with a love eternal, he was on a equal footing with me in my house. I told him every step I made, and all my spiritual possessions were at his disposal, because nothing was hidden from his spirit thirsting after knowledge. And as he used to come to my house every morning, very early, swift and light as a deer, to learn the words of the living God, he searched all through my library, found there some of my writings which God granted me, then crossed even the stream of Kabbalah, and also tasted of the Tree of Life (the book by Chaim Vital, disciple of the Ari). Then his mind began to wander in the valley of mysticism, and began to love it and to enjoy it."

THE REVEREND EZRA STILES
(1727-1795)

Ezra Stiles was president of Yale College between 1778 and 1795, during the historic period when the United States of America was founded. Stiles, considered the most learned scholar in all of New England, was a Congregational clergyman, scientist, and theologian who studied and practiced law for a few years before returning to ministry. Stiles staunchly supported the American Revolutionary cause and placed great value on education, religion, and science. Benjamin Franklin was a friend of Ezra Stiles, and they corresponded on a regular basis. In fact, Franklin sent Stiles various pieces of scientific equipment so that he could conduct electrical experiments while at Yale University.

Stiles believed deeply that America would excel in all areas because the country was founded upon religion, and would, therefore, receive the appropriate blessings in return. In 1773, Stiles befriended the Sephardic Rabbi Raphael Haim Isaac Carigal, who wound up having a significant influence on the development of Yale University in the late 1700s. Carigal instructed Stiles in Hebrew, helping him become a Hebrew scholar, and Carigal nurtured in Stiles a fascination with the *Zohar* and kabbalistic wisdom. Carigal also delivered and published the first ever rabbinical sermon in America on May 28 in 1773, three years before the United States was officially founded. It was on the holiday of Shavuot, which commemorates the actual date of the Revelation event on Mount Sinai.

Stiles learned about the *Zohar* from other rabbis as well, and devoted much of his personal time to studying the texts of *Zohar*, as indicated by his own diary entries.

- *November 25th, studying the Zohar all day*

- *In the Afternoon Rabbi Moses came to my house in company with Huzan Touro of this Town. We had much conversation both of his Travels and on the Talmud and Rabbinical Literature. I showed him the Zohar, with which he was delighted, speaking with raptures of the Sublimity and Mysteries of its Contents; he told me if I could comprehend that Book I should be a Master of the Jewish Learning and of the greatest philosophy in the World*

- *Visited this Afternoon by Rabbi Tobiah Bar Jehudah late from near Cracow in Poland set. We had much Conversation on the Zohar*

- *Lately I have made much use of the Zohar in which with the Syriac I now daily read a portion.*

  The Literary Diary of Ezra Stiles
  By Ezra Stiles
  Published by C. Scribner's sons, 1901
  Item notes: v.1
  Original from Harvard University Digitized
  Oct 31, 2006

Stiles's fascination with the *Zohar* and Hebrew is reflected in Yale's official seal where the Hebrew words: "*Urim*" and "*Tumim*," are displayed with equal prominence as the Latin "*Lux et Veritas*" — translated as Light and Truth. Hebrew also became a required course in the Yale curriculum.

THOMAS ALVA EDISON
(1847-1931)

Thomas Alva Edison also drew on Kabbalah and shared its views on the fundamental nature of reality. Edison believed that all of his inventions pre-existed in a higher reality, akin to the 99 percent in Kabbalah, or Plato's World of Ideas. Edison's mystical bent is discussed by Robert Conot in his book *A Streak of Luck: The Life of Thomas.* Conot states: "Through much of his life Edison was attracted by mysticism. After the phonograph came into existence, he could almost sense a mystic force moving about in the Universe."

Like Leibniz, Edison believed that the building blocks of reality were not physical entities but rather fields of energy imbued with consciousness, and thus were the source of human consciousness. In an interview with Harpers Magazine, Edison discussed his belief that atoms were imbued with conscious thought:

> *"I do not believe that matter is inert, acted upon by an outside force. To me it seems that every atom is possessed by a certain amount of primitive intelligence: look at the thousand ways in which atoms of hydrogen combine with those of other elements.... Do you mean to say they do this without intelligence?"*

In an article in Scientific American in 1920, we discover that Edison's belief in conscious atoms was questioned by the interviewer who asked from where do atoms receive their intelligence. Edison replied *"From some power greater than us."* Edison went on to say that chemistry could, indeed, prove the existence of God.

In 1878, Thomas Alva Edison joined the Theosophical Society and signed its pledge of secrecy. Dr. Seth Pancoast was the organization's vice-president, and the controversial psychic and medium Helena P. Blavatsky was president. It is clear that kabbalistic ideas permeated this group. Not only did Blavatsky make this clear in her writings, but Pancoast did as well.

After describing Pythagoras as *"a kabbalist of the highest order,"* Pancoast goes on to discuss Pythagoras' belief that the numbers 10 and 4 were the perfect numbers, as articulated by the ancient philosopher Aetius in the first century AD.

> *"Ten is the very nature of number. All Greeks and all barbarians alike count up to ten, and having reached ten revert again to the unity. And again, Pythagoras maintains, the power of the number 10 lies in the number 4, the tetrad. This is the reason: if one starts at the unit (1) and adds the successive number up to 4, one will make up the number 10 (1+2+3+4 = 10). And if one exceeds the tetrad, one will exceed 10 too.... So that the number by the unit resides in the number 10, but potentially in the number 4. And so the Pythagoreans used to invoke the Tetrad as their most binding oath: 'By him that gave to our generation the Tetractys, which contains the fount and root of eternal nature....'"*

Pancoast then draws stunning parallels between Pythagorean belief and the Tetragrammaton, the sacred four-letter Name of God (יְהֹוָה) and the Ten *Sefirot* of kabbalistic cosmology. Pancoast writes:

> *"The Greek alchemist Pythagoras correctly regarded the Ineffable Name of God—the Tetragrammaton or Four Letter Name—as the key to the mysteries of the Universe and of its creation and preservation. This is the Name that so many have sought, that they might unlock the mystical secrets of Magic, discover the treasures of Symbolism, and fathom the depths of All Learning and Wisdom.... Now Pythagoras, a great and singularly learned man, took the four letters of the Tetragrammaton and, arranging them as a pyramid or cone within a double circle, derived the ten numbers of creation from them. These ten numbers represent the principles of all things."*

Pancoast adds: *"the hidden ways of wisdom are in the Ten Sefirot."*

The kabbalists and the *Zohar* concur with this view by assigning each of the Ten *Sefirot* to one of the Four Letters of the Tetragrammaton. *Keter,* the crown of the Universe, correlates to the very tip of the letter *Yud. Chochmah* is embodied by the rest of the body of the *Yud. Binah* is assigned to the letter *Hei.* The six *Sefirot* of *Chesed, Gevurah, Tiferet, Netzach, Hod* and *Yesod* (*Zeir Anpin*) are included in the letter *Vav.* And our physical realm of *Malchut,* the lowest sphere, is manifested in the final letter *Hei.* Thus the four letters contain the ten.

The Pythagorean Tetractys (illustrated below) further refers to the *72 Names of God* as discussed in the *Zohar.* By adding up the numerical value of each Hebrew letter appearing in Pythagoras' Tetractys, each of the four rows, the sum total equals 72.

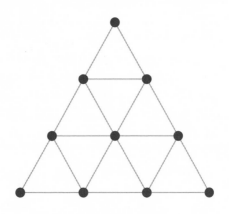

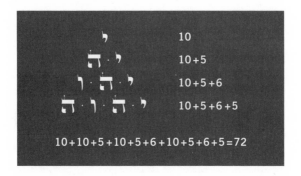

BRIGADIER GENERAL
ALBERT PIKE
(1809-1891)

Albert Pike holds the distinction of being the only Confederate General with a monument on Federal property in Washington DC. The statue honoring Pike sits thirteen blocks from the White House in Judiciary Square. Pike was a renowned journalist, a prominent Washington DC lawyer, a social reformer, and the Sovereign Grand Commander of the Scottish Rite Freemasons. His friends included Davey Crockett, and he was unquestionably one of the most popular dinner guests in Washington society.

From time to time throughout American history, Freemasons have held the highest office in the land. American Presidents who were Freemasons include George Washington, Andrew Johnson,

Theodore Roosevelt, Franklin Roosevelt, Harry Truman, Lyndon Johnson, and Gerald Ford. As a 33rd degree Mason and the Grand Commander, Albert Pike was the highest-ranking Mason of his time.

On April 9, 1898, the United States Congress authorized the placement of the Albert Pike monument, thirteen blocks from the White House, outside the headquarters of the Southern Jurisdiction of the Scottish Rite in Washington, D.C. Above it is a quote from General Pike, which conveys the essence of kabbalistic teachings:

> *"What we have done for ourselves alone dies with us; what we have done for others and the world remains and is immortal."*

There is something unique about the monument honoring Albert Pike. The General is holding a book in his hand. It's called *Morals and Dogma*. The book, written by Pike, is considered to be the *Bible* of the Scottish Rite Freemasons. Only those masons who attained the highest degree were awarded this secret book.

In *Morals and Dogma*, General Pike cast light on the mysterious origins of the Freemasons, and he revealed a tightly guarded secret concerning the source of all wisdom and the true origins of Christianity. What follows are quotes from his book.

> *"Masonry is a search after Light. That search leads us directly back to the Kabbalah!"*

> *"All Masonic associations owe Kabbalah their secrets and their symbols."*

> *"One is filled with admiration, on penetrating into the Sanctuary of the Kabbalah, at seeing a doctrine so logical, so simple, and at the same time so absolute."*

> *"The Zohar...the key of the Holy Books, opens up all the depths and lights, all the obscurities of the Ancient Mythologies and of the Sciences.*

> *"All religions have issued from Kabbalah and return to it."*

Regarding the true origins of Christianity Pike wrote:

> *"Christ himself, recognized it as a truth, that all Scripture had an inner and an outer meaning."*

> *"Paul studied Kabbalah at the feet of Gamaliel the Rabbi."*

> *"Here is the origin of the Trinity, of the Father, the Mother or Holy Spirit, and the Son."*

On the origins of the wisdom of Pythagoras, Pike wrote:

> *"Pythagoras visited all the sanctuaries of the world. He went into Judea, where he procured himself to be circumcised, that he might be admitted to the secrets of the Kabbalah, which the prophets Ezekiel and Daniel communicated to him."*

RAV YEHUDA HALEVY ASHLAG
(1885-1954)

He has been called the most profound kabbalist of the 20th century, but he is perhaps best known for casting off Kabbalah's shroud of secrecy. The eminent Kabbalist and revered master, Rav Yehuda Ashlag, broke with the two thousand-year-old tradition that had locked Kabbalah's great power inside the mystifying writings of the *Zohar* and the *Writings of the Ari*. As far as this renowned Kabbalist was concerned, the time had come to change all that. The ancient vaults to Kabbalah were opened wide by this renowned sage, for he was convinced that there was no longer any danger associated with exposing Kabbalah's secret lore to the masses.

In his kabbalistic treatise *Entrance to the Tree of Life*, Rav Ashlag explained that the *Zohar* foresaw modern materialism and its dominance over spiritual reality. During such times, people motivated by self-interest, intellectualism, and ego would avoid spiritual wisdom like the plague. Only those who sought out truth with a pure heart would be able to find this wisdom. Therefore, according to Rav Ashlag, there would be no risk in revealing the innermost secrets of the *Zohar*.

In his zeal to share the secrets of Kabbalah, Rav Ashlag would manage to write eighteen hours a day, often on scraps of paper due to his dire financial situation. In 1922 he established the first Kabbalah Centre, in the city of Jerusalem. Learning was made available to those who were steeped in religious studies, Orthodox, and over the age of forty. Many leading rabbis of his generation applauded this historic opening, and including Rabbi Abraham Isaac Kook, Chief Rabbi of Israel.

Rav Ashlag delved into Lurianic Kabbalah with devout fervor. He unraveled prolific kabbalistic secrets and recorded them in his monumental work *The Writings of the Ari*, bringing order and structure to Lurianic Kabbalah. His penetrating commentary of the *Zohar*, known as the *Sulam* (the Ladder), was the first ever complete translation of the *Zohar* into Modern Hebrew. Still, the vast majority of the world paid little attention to this historic action, nor could they perceive its influence. Only in the early 21st century have both scholars and lay people begun to recognize the genius of Rav Ashlag, and the historic nature of his contributions.

Concepts such as relativity, the space-time continuum, the role of spirit in healing, and other matters affecting the welfare of humankind were all alluded to in the *Zohar*. Rav Ashlag's genius lay in his ability to extrapolate these secrets from the Ari's 500-year-old writings and the texts of the *Zohar*. His efforts influenced the technological explosion of the 20th century, much the same way Lurianic Kabbalah impacted the scientific revolution of the 17th century. Rav Ashlag passed on during the Day of Atonement (Yom Kippur) in 1955.

RAV YEHUDA TZVI BRANDWEIN
(1904-1969)

Rav Ashlag's disciple and successor, Kabbalist Rav Yehuda Tzvi Brandwein (1904-1969), helped complete and publish Rav Ashlag's monumental Hebrew translation and commentary. Rav Brandwein was a unique and gentle soul who became the Chief Rabbi of the one-million-member *Histadrut* (Labor Union) in Israel. His tolerant kabbalistic way of life, which was based on unconditional love regardless of faith and practice, was what motivated a non-religious organization like Histadrut to select an orthodox kabbalist as its Chief Rabbi. Rav Brandwein believed—as did the kabbalists before him, that the dissemination of the *Zohar* would remove the religious persecutions and bloodshed that had marked the landscape of humankind for thousands of years. Rav Brandwein believed this would happen once the *Zohar*'s rich and deep texts were made comprehensible to the common person.

RAV PHILIP BERG
(1927-   )

Rav Brandwein's disciple and successor, Kabbalist Rav Philip Berg brought to fruition the goal of his teacher and his teacher's teacher by publishing

The Writings of the Ari and the *Sulam* edition of the *Zohar* in the 1970's and 80's. Close to three hundred thousand sets of *The Writings of the Ari* and a half a million volumes of the *Zohar* with *Ma'alot haSulam* and *Sulam* commentaries made it, at that time, the largest production and dissemination of *Zoharic* and Lurianic Kabbalistic texts since the inception of the printing press and thus, in all of history.

MODERN DAY PARALLELS

"When I read that a stone consisted of trillions of molecules constantly in motion and that these molecules consisted of atoms and that these atoms were in themselves complicated systems, whirls of energy, I said to myself "That's the Kabbalah after all!"
—Isaac Bashevis Singer, Winner, 1978, Nobel Prize in Literature

With the advent of 20th century physics, and the historic dissemination of the *Zohar*, correlations between Kabbalah and contemporary cosmology and medical science increasingly attracted public attention.

For instance, Plato's teachings have been among the most influential in the history of Western civilization. Plato contemplated an independent reality of Ideas as the only guarantee of objective scientific knowledge. Plato postulated a theory of Ideas and Forms, and only these Ideas were completely real.

Sir Roger Penrose, Royal Society member and eminent Oxford mathematical physicist, one of the great experts of our day on the makeup of the Universe, says in his book *Shadows of the Mind:*

> *"According to Plato, mathematical concepts and truths inhabit an actual world of their own that is timeless and without physical location. Plato's world is an ideal world of perfect forms, distinct from the physical world...."*

As shown earlier, the greatest scientist ever, Sir Isaac Newton, concluded that Plato liberated these remarkable notions from the wisdom of Kabbalah, whose teachings offer identical and even more comprehensive insights into this concept.

For example, from the perspective of Kabbalah, the physical world that we perceive through the five senses embodies a mere 1 percent of absolute reality. The remaining 99 percent exists in other dimensions (*Sefirot*) beyond the realm of physical matter. Physical reality is merely a reflection or shadow of the higher supernal world, which is the source of all wisdom, happiness, and creativity. A metaphysical curtain separates these two realms. Professor Stuart Hameroff, Ph.D., along with Sir Roger Penrose developed *The Penrose-Hameroff 'Orch OR' Model of Consciousness*. Dr. Hameroff was intrigued by Kabbalah's description of reality, specifically the 1 percent and 99 percent realities.

Hameroff states:

> *"For 100 years it has been known that there exist two worlds, the classical world and the quantum world. We live in the classical world where everything seems "normal" (if unfulfilling). Everything has a definite shape, place and substance. However at very small scales the quantum world reigns, and everything is strange and bizarre, defying common sense. Science knows very little about the quantum world, but there are indications that the quantum world could qualify as the 99% reality, and that a curtain does indeed exist between the two worlds."*

Theoretical physicist Fred Alan Wolf notes the parallels between Kabbalah and science, saying, *"This is a case where scientists may be proving what mystics have revealed through different means."*

THE END OF HISTORY

As more books are being written about the *Zohar*, exciting ideas such as nanotechnology, cold fusion, teleportation, stem cells, parallel Universes and other cutting edge concepts are emerging from its text, promoting what the kabbalists for centuries have promised—the reconciliation of the *Zohar* with science, providing mankind with a complete picture of the spiritual and physical realities and the metaphysical and physical laws that govern both realms. As the Kabbalist Moshe Chaim Luzzatto stated in the 18th century, each new generation merits uncovering another layer of *Zoharic* wisdom, thereby contributing to the restoration of the world and the revelation of the *Or HaGanuz* (Hidden Light) that was lost on Mount Sinai as a result of the golden calf.

Thus it becomes clear that the *Zohar's* emergence in the 21st century, along with a deeper understanding of its profound influence in history and the discovery of the latest scientific and medical secrets concealed within its texts, is providing us with an unprecedented opportunity to remove the darkness and chaos that has ravaged the landscape of human civilization for millennia.

The history of the *Zohar* continues to be written even as these words are being set down, and read; each sentence brings you, me, and the whole world one step closer to the Final Redemption. For the first time in history, the *Zohar* has been printed on a scale that has allowed millions of copies to be disseminated around the world through an unprecedented number of outreach programs, and educational and spiritual projects.

As this brief volume comes to a close, I am reminded that the greatest moments in the story of the *Zohar* lie ahead; it is my profound wish that they may come soon, for you and for all to share. May the Final Redemption now dawn with infinite sweetness and mercy, for therein lies the ultimate power and purpose of the *Zohar*, the magnificent *Book of Splendor.*

SECRET HISTORY OF THE ZOHAR

TIMELINE

The events noted in this book begin with Moses and the Revelation at Mount Sinai where the Light of the *Zohar* was referred to as the *Or HaGanuz* (Hidden Light).

Pythagoras (569 BCE-475 BCE) and Plato: According to Hermippus of Smyrna, the third century philosopher, Pythagoras owed all of his theories to the Jews. He accused Pythagoras of imitating the doctrines of the Jews and transferring them into his own philosophy.

50-135 CE: Rabbi Akiva was the greatest soul to appear in the physical realm and teacher to Rabbi Shimon bar Yochai.

70 CE: Destruction of the Second Temple.

100-160 CE: Rabbi Shimon bar Yochai was chosen to reveal the *Zohar*. He and Rabbi Elazar, his son, hid in the ground, in a cave for 13 years. Rabbi Abba concealed the wisdom in writing the physical book of the *Zohar*.

121-180 CE: Rabbi Shimon bar Yochai was visiting Rome when the Roman Emperor Marcus Aurelius' daughter fell ill, Rabbi Shimon bar Yochai healed her and, in turn, a set of decrees issued against the Israelites by Rome was annulled.

1040-1105: Rabbi Shlomo Yitzhaki (Rashi), famed as the author of the first comprehensive commentaries on the Torah, points out that the word used in the Torah to describe the veil that conceals this beaming *Zoharic* radiance of Moses' countenance is actually an Aramaic word (*masveh*)—not Hebrew. Here we have an Aramaic veil concealing a Divine Light that is referred to as *Zohar*, a precise parallel itself to the Aramaic book called *Zohar*.

1093-1167: Medieval kabbalist and astronomer Rabbi Abraham Ibn Ezra points out that Moses' face radiated after receiving the second Tablets; a phenomenon that did not occur with the first Tablets. Moreover, Rabbi Ibn Ezra utilizes the word *Zohar* to describe the Light on Moses' face.

Until the **1200s**, the *Zohar* lay concealed. Many, including Pope Innocent III, Rabbi Abraham ben David and Joachim of Fiore, predicted the Messiah and the Final Redemption to occur around this time.

1290: Moses De Leon publishes *Zohar* booklets for distribution. Rabbi Joseph Halevi tested De Leon. He claimed that he lost his copy of the manuscript and asked De Leon to write him a new one. De Leon reproduced it exactly.

14th-17th Century: The Renaissance: The influence of the *Zohar*, Rabbi Shimon, and the emergence of Kabbalah in the Middle Ages can be seen to this very day. The Christian scholars, philosophers, and scientists during the Renaissance and the age of Scientific Revolution were students of kabbalists.

1450-1510: Rabbi Avraham Zacuto's *Sefer Yuhasin* (*Book of Geneologies*) contains "a single fragmentary piece of evidence" concerning the origins of the *Zohar*. This evidence comes in the form of testimony by the Kabbalist Rabbi Isaac of Acre, in the thirteenth century, who was so moved by the heavenly power of the *Zohar*'s text that he traveled to Toledo to inquire about its origins. Rabbi Isaac said that the Hebrew sections of the *Zohar* were forged and that the Aramaic verses were from the hand of Rabbi Shimon bar Yochai.

1455-1522: Johannes Reuchlin delved into kabbalistic study with great fervor, producing written works in which he credited Kabbalah as the prime influence and source of wisdom for the great minds of history, including Pythagoras. He believed that all Christians should learn Aramaic and Hebrew so that they could study the *Zohar* and other great kabbalistic texts.

1463-1494: Count Giovanni Pico della Mirandola of Florence is generally credited with injecting the mystical teachings of kabbalistic wisdom into the very nucleus of the Italian Renaissance, planting a seed that would blossom into what became a sudden eruption of scientific advancement and discovery.

1475-1564: Michelangelo lived with and was supported by the famous Medici family. Lorenzo Medici literally controlled the city and he gathered together great minds and great artists, many of whom studied the *Zohar* to help enrich Florence.

1492: Christopher Columbus and Rabbi Abraham Zacuto were influenced by the *Zohar*, with its mention of a round world.

1492: After the expulsion of the Jews from Spain, the fountainhead of kabbalistic activity moved to the mystical town of Safed, located in Northern Israel amid the historic mountains of Galilee.

1493-1541: Paracelsus credits the ancient teachings of Kabbalah as the foundation of his and all knowledge.

1527-1608: John Dee, one of the most brilliant minds during the age of Queen Elizabeth 1, was proficient as a renowned mathematician, geographer, astronomer, astrologer, scientist, and personal adviser to Queen Elizabeth. According to Deborah Harkness, Professor of History at the University of Southern California, Dee was convinced that Kabbalah could reveal the hidden truth about the natural world through hidden messages that God embedded into this physical reality. He looked to Kabbalah as the singular way to reconcile and unite all the physical laws of the natural world with the spiritual laws that govern the metaphysical reality.

1534-1572: Rabbi Isaac Luria (the Ari) lived in Sefad where he decoded the *Zohar* through his famous discourses. The Ari's teachings had a profound effect that contributed significantly to the Scientific Revolution.

1543-1620: Rabbi Chaim Vital, the Ari's disciple, committed the Ari's oral teaching to writings with his son Rabbi Shmuel Vital, thus giving birth to what is now known as Lurianic Kabbalah.

1559: The *Zohar* was printed for the very first time. Ironically, it was the Catholic Church that contributed to the broad circulation of the *Zohar* and kabbalistic wisdom. At a time when the Roman Inquisition and the destruction of Jewish books were taking place, Pope Paul IV (1476-1559) himself gave his approval to the publication of the *Zohar*, which rolled off the printing presses.

16th-17th Century: The *Zohar* had a profound influence on many of the greatest scientists and mathematicians of the 16th and 17th centuries—a time when the lines between philosophy and science, physics and metaphysics, were virtually non-existent.

1643-1727: Sir Isaac Newton's view of the Bible as a cosmic code or cryptogram was congruent with the views of the kabbalists throughout history. It's worth noting that Newton went to the trouble of learning the Hebrew language so that he could extract these great kabbalistic secrets from the scriptures.

1646-1716: 17th-centruy German scientist Gottfried Leibniz was introduced to Kabbalah by Francis van Helmont, the editor of the Latin translation of the *Zohar, Kabbalah Denudata,* which profoundly influenced Leibniz's philosophy and views concerning the nature of reality and the structure of the cosmos.

1684: Knorr von Rosenroth translated the *Zohar* and the writings of Kabbalist Rabbi Isaac Luria into Latin, producing *Kabbalah Denudata* (Kabbalah Unveiled). Like Pico and Reuchlin, von Rosenroth considered Kabbalah to be the true ancient wisdom given to Moses on Mount Sinai.

1707-1746: Rabbi Moshe Chaim Luzzatto (the Ramchal) worked on a Second *Zohar*, which delves deeper into the secrets hidden inside the *Zohar*, but had to bury his writings (or have them burned by Christians) because of threats from rabbis of his day.

1727-1795: Reverend Ezra Stiles was president of Yale College between 1778 and 1795. In 1773, Stiles befriended the Sephardic Rabbi Raphael Haim Isaac Carigal who instructed Stiles in Hebrew,and was amongst a few rabbis who nurtured in Stiles a fascination with the *Zohar* and kabbalistic wisdom.

May 28, 1773: Rabbi Carigal also delivered and published the first ever rabbinical sermon in America, three years before the United States was officially founded. It was on the holiday of *Shavuot*, which commemorates the actual date of the Revelation event on Mount Sinai.

1724-1807: Rabbi Hayim Joseph David Azulai (the Chidah) in his manuscript, *Shem haGedolim*, states there is yet another version of the origins of the *Zohar*, which concerns a king who ordered an excavation in search of treasure, but instead found the *Zohar*. It was brought to the wise men of Christendom, who failed to decipher it. So they brought the enigmatic manuscript to the hub of kabbalistic study, Toledo, Spain, where it came into the hands of Moses De Leon.

1809-1891: In *Morals and Dogma*, Brigadier General Albert Pike cast light on the mysterious origins of the Freemasons, and he revealed a tightly guarded secret concerning the source of all wisdom and the true origins of Christianity, quoting: *"All religions have issued from Kabbalah and return to it."*

Rabbi Joseph Halevi tested De Leon. He claimed that he lost his copy of the *Zohar* manuscript and asked De Leon to write him a new one. De Leon reproduced it exactly.

1847-1931: Thomas Alva Edison also drew on Kabbalah and shared its views on the fundamental nature of reality. Edison believed that the building blocks of reality were not physical entities but rather fields of energy imbued with consciousness, and thus were the source of human consciousness. He said that chemistry could, indeed, prove the existence of God. Edison joined the Theosophical Society whose members studied Kabbalah and the *Zohar*.

1885-1954: Rav Ashlag opened the first ever Kabbalah Centre in Jerusalem in 1922. Rav Ashlag decided it was time that Kabbalah and *Zohar* were revealed to everyone and wrote the *Sulam* to the *Zohar*.

1904-1969: Rav Ashlag's disciple and successor, Rav Yehuda Tzvi Brandwein, helped complete and publish Rav Ashlag's monumental Hebrew translation and commentary. Rav Brandwein believed—as did the kabbalists before him—that the dissemination of the Zohar would remove the religious persecutions and bloodshed that had marked the landscape of humankind for thousands of years. And this would happen once the *Zohar*'s rich and deep texts were made comprehensible to the common person.

1962: Max I. Dimont, in his book *Jews, God and History*, considered the role of the *Zohar* as a possible scientific catalyst. Evidence pointing to a kabbalistic connection with the likes of Sir Isaac Newton, Wilhelm Leibniz, and others had not yet emerged.

1969: Kabbalist Rav Philip Berg became director of The Kabbalah Centre, assuming leadership from his master and teacher Rav Brandwein. Rav Berg brought to fruition the goal of his teacher and his teacher's teacher by publishing *The Writings of the Ari* and the *Sulam* edition of the *Zohar* in the 1970's and 80's. Close to three hundred thousand sets of *The Writings of the Ari* and a half a million volumes of the *Zohar* with *Ma'a lot haSulam* and *Sulam* commentaries made it, at that time, the largest production and dissemination of *Zoharic* and Lurianic Kabbalistic texts since the inception of the printing press and thus, in all of history.

Today: there are millions of sets of the *Zohar* currently in circulation worldwide.

The End of History: promising the Final Redemption, with the mass dissemination of the *Zohar* and its secrets to all of humanity.

INDEX

Secrets of the Zohar: Stories and Meditations to Awaken the Heart
By Michael Berg

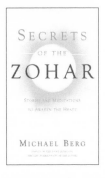

The *Zohar*'s secrets are the secrets of the Bible, passed on as oral tradition and then recorded as a sacred text that remained hidden for thousands of years. They have never been revealed quite as they are here in these pages, which decipher the codes behind the best stories of the ancient sages and offer a special meditation for each one. Entire portions of the *Zohar* are presented, with the Aramaic and its English translation in side-by-side columns. This allows you to scan and to read aloud so that you can draw on the *Zohar*'s full energy and achieve spiritual transformation. Open this book and open your heart to the Light of the *Zohar*!

The Wisdom of Truth: 12 Essays by the Holy Kabbalist Rav Yehuda Ashlag
Edited by Michael Berg

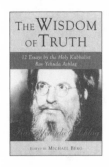

The 12 essays presented here are remarkable in that they cover and condense all of the basic truths of Kabbalah. Essentially, the essays are about human dignity and how people must behave toward one another in order to eliminate chaos in the world, based on the abiding principle of "Love Thy Neighbor as Thyself." Rav Ashlag understood that the transformation of human consciousness from a state of desiring to receive to desiring to give—that is, from greed and selfishness to love and sharing—is the true challenge of humankind.

116

The Secret: Unlocking the Source of Joy & Fulfillment
By Michael Berg

The Secret reveals the essence of life in its most concise and powerful form. Several years before the latest "Secret" phenomenon, Michael Berg shared the amazing truths of the world's oldest spiritual wisdom in this book. In it, he has pieced together an ancient puzzle to show that our common understanding of life's purpose is actually backwards, and that anything less than complete joy and fulfillment can be changed by correcting this misperception.

Nano: Technology of Mind over Matter
By Rav Berg

Kabbalah is all about attaining control over the physical world, including our personal lives, at the most fundamental level of reality. It's about achieving and extending mind over matter and developing the ability to create fulfillment, joy, and happiness by controlling everything at the most basic level of existence.

In this way, Kabbalah predates and presages the most exciting trend in recent scientific and technological development, the application of nano-technology to all areas of life in order to create better, stronger, and more efficient results.

In his latest and perhaps most brilliant work, one of the greatest kabbalists of our time demystifies the connection between the ancient wisdom of Kabbalah and current scientific thought, and shows how the union of the two will bring about the end of chaos in the foreseeable future.

The Way of the Kabbalist: A User's Guide to Technology for the Soul™
By Yehuda Berg

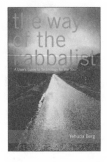

Everything you ever wanted to know about the spiritual technology taught by The Kabbalah Centre is defined and explained in this book.

Learn the kabbalistic secrets behind the cycles of life, birth, and death, marriage and sex, the difference between men and women, and the significance of certain colors, foods, hair, and red string, as well as the energies of special days, weeks, and holidays.

What might seem like mysterious rituals to the uninformed are actually practical tools and meditations that all of us can use to connect with the Light to achieve positive goals and total fulfillment—and, ultimately, global transformation.

The 72 Names of God: Technology for the Soul™
By Yehuda Berg

The 72 Names of God are not "names" in any ordinary sense, but a state-of-the-art technology that deeply touches the human soul and is the key to ridding yourself of depression, stress, stagnation, anger, and many other emotional and physical problems. The Names represent a connection to the infinite spiritual current that flows through the universe. When you correctly bring these power sources together, you are able to gain control over your life and transform it for the better.

THE ZOHAR

Composed more than 2,000 years ago, the *Zohar* is a set of 23 books, a commentary on biblical and spiritual matters in the form of conversations among spiritual masters. But to describe the *Zohar* only in physical terms is greatly misleading. In truth, the *Zohar* is nothing less than a powerful tool for achieving the most important purposes of our lives. It was given to all humankind by the Creator to bring us protection, to connect us with the Creator's Light, and ultimately to fulfill our birthright of true spiritual transformation.

More than eighty years ago, when The Kabbalah Centre was founded, the *Zohar* had virtually disappeared from the world. Few people in the general population had ever heard of it. Whoever sought to read it—in any country, in any language, at any price—faced a long and futile search.

Today all this has changed. Through the work of The Kabbalah Centre and the editorial efforts of Michael Berg, the *Zohar* is now being brought to the world, not only in the original Aramaic language but also in English. The new English *Zohar* provides everything for connecting to this sacred text on all levels: the original Aramaic text for scanning; an English translation; and clear, concise commentary for study and learning.

THE KABBALAH CENTRE®

The Kabbalah Centre® is a spiritual organization dedicated to bringing the wisdom of Kabbalah to the world. The Kabbalah Centre® itself has existed for more than 80 years, but its spiritual lineage extends back to Rav Isaac Luria in the 16th century and even further back to Rav Shimon bar Yochai, who revealed the principal text of Kabbalah, the Zohar, more than 2,000 years ago.

The Kabbalah Centre® was founded in 1922 by Rav Yehuda Ashlag, one of the greatest kabbalists of the 20th Century. When Rav Ashlag left this world, leadership of The Kabbalah Centre® was taken on by Rav Yehuda Brandwein. Before his passing, Rav Brandwein designated Rav Berg as director of The Kabbalah Centre®. Now, for more than 30 years, The Kabbalah Centre® has been under the direction of Rav Berg, his wife Karen Berg, and their sons, Yehuda Berg and Michael Berg.

Although there are many scholarly studies of Kabbalah, The Kabbalah Centre® does not teach Kabbalah as an academic discipline but as a way of creating a better life. The mission of The Kabbalah Centre® is to make the practical tools and spiritual teachings of Kabbalah available and accessible to everyone regardless of religion, ethnicity, gender or age.

The Kabbalah Centre® makes no promises. But if people are willing to work hard to grow and become actively sharing, caring and tolerant human beings, Kabbalah teaches that they will then experience fulfillment and joy in a way previously unknown to them. This sense of fulfillment, however, comes gradually and is always the result of the student's spiritual work.

Our ultimate goal is for all humanity to gain the happiness and fulfillment that is our true destiny.

Kabbalah teaches its students to question and test everything they learn. One of the most important teachings of Kabbalah is that there is no coercion in spirituality.

What Does The Kabbalah Centre® Offer?

Local Kabbalah Centres around the world offer onsite lectures, classes, study groups, holiday celebrations and services, and a community of teachers and fellow students. To find a Centre near you, go to www.kabbalah.com.

For those of you unable to access a physical Kabbalah Centre due to the constraints of location or time, we have other ways to participate in The Kabbalah Centre® community.

At www.kabbalah.com, we feature online blogs, newsletters, weekly wisdom, a store, and much more.

It's a wonderful way to stay tuned in and in touch, and it gives you access to programs that will expand your mind and challenge you to continue your spiritual work.

Student Support

The Kabbalah Centre® empowers people to take responsibility for their own lives. It's about the teachings, not the teachers. But on your journey to personal growth, things can be unclear and sometimes rocky, so it is helpful to have a coach or teacher. Simply call 1 800 KABBALAH toll free.

In appreciation of our teachers;
the Rav and Karen and the entire family

May infinite Love and Light be revealed
to the world.

Elizabeth and Steve